IN TIMES OF TROUBLE

Volume III

Stories of God's Help in Time of Need

All stories are presented in the first person but were compiled and written by the following members of Foothills Church:

Roxanne Fulkerson
Wes Fulkerson
Brian Hilemon
Jim Self
Jenny Stecklair
General Editor: Wes Fulkerson
Line Editor: Allison Schutz

In Times of Trouble Volume III:
Stories of God's Help in Time of Need

Table of Contents

Editor's Note:

The following stories are true accounts of real people living, learning, and walking with the Lord. If any of these testimonies touch your heart and you need someone to talk to, please reach out to the church office so you can be connected to one of our pastors or the resources you need.

If you are struggling with anxiety, depression, hard financial circumstances, or any other hardship, know that the church is here to help and provide the love of Christ. No one should walk alone.

Foothills Christian Church Office:
(619) 442-7728
Receptionist@foothillschurch.org

Foothills Christian Church Counseling Office:
(619) 442-7728 (ask for Counseling)
Counseling@foothillschurch.org

<u>Church Office</u>
350 Cypress Lane, Ste. B
El Cajon, CA 92020

<u>Sanctuary</u>
365 W. Bradley Ave.
El Cajon, CA 92020

Linda Quiroz

"Proof that God Can Save Anyone"

I have to tell you, I am a walking miracle – proof that God can save and redeem anyone.

God has protected my life so many times, when, by rights, I should have died an early death or ended up in an institution. My mother set fire to our house with my baby brother and me still inside. She left us on a street corner in New York City when I was three years old. We wound up in a foster home run by a pedophile.

How's that for a beginning to a life? I have walked in abandonment, phobias of people and outdoors. I have lived through sleepless nights full of nightmares and voices. I have been involved with cults. I have been a thief, a liar, self-absorbed, and full of self-hatred. Hatred, anger, rage, and alcoholism were my friends. I tried to commit suicide at the age of five.

You might ask, "How does a person climb out of such calamity?" God sent people to help. The first time I encountered God was when I got put on a bus to go to a Christian camp being held for poor kids. The pastor there told us the following story about Niagara Falls:

A world-renowned tightrope walker set up a line across the Niagara Falls drop-off and walked across, then ran, then finally cartwheeled across. The crowd went wild as he stepped off the line to retrieve a wheelbarrow, which he then placed on the tightrope. "Do you believe I can push this wheelbarrow across this wire?" he asked. The crowd unanimously cheered and shouted that they believed he could. "How sure are you?" "Positive! Certain! You can do it!" the crowd cried. "Since you have such confidence in me," the tightrope walker began, "I'll need someone to get in so I can push it across." That quieted the onlookers. You see, believing the performer had the skill was one thing, but putting faith in him was another. People were afraid even though he had demonstrated his ability again and again. Someone finally stepped forward, the performer pushed him across, and the people cheered as they glanced down at the deadly fall.

I was only in the fifth grade when I heard the pastor tell this story, and I related to the wild and dangerous setting – my whole life felt like I was looking over the edge of a waterfall. But I knew that I wanted to be in the hands of someone who was safe with me, even in that chaos. I wanted to be in the wheelbarrow.

I stood up to receive Christ, as my friend pulled on my arm to try and make me sit down.

I still had a long, painful, sin-filled road to go down. I didn't walk with the Lord for many years after this first conversion, but it's funny; no matter how hard I tried to pull away from my commitment to God, He always pulled me back. I would be tempted to think, "I was just a kid!" but I imagine God saying, "Oh well. I took you seriously, so I'm going to keep after you."

I lived a dark life, spiraling down until age 21, when my birth mom invited me to a charismatic conference. It was a Catholic charismatic renewal event, and these people were serious about Jesus. The priest said that if we prayed to God, "Jesus, I give You my life. I need Your help," that He would come into our hearts. Well, I did need help. I was at a real low-point – depressed, mean as a cuss to anyone and everyone who had the misfortune of crossing my path, and I hated where I was in life, full of anger and confusion. I prayed to accept Christ, and He really came into my heart that day. I had a long bus ride back home from the conference, and the whole way I heard the Lord whispering to my heart, "I love you. I love you. I love you." When I got off that bus, I was on fire to share this great news! I told everybody, "Hey! Did you know God loves you? He loves you!" To this day, it's one of my sweetest memories.

Growing and healing was a process, of course, but God never left my side. He put a Christian woman in my life who taught me to pray. I prayed for God's help, and He miraculously watched over my life.

He has healed me from cancer, alcoholism, self-mutilation, and fear. The individual stories would take too long to write in this short space, but please – come find me and ask me about them. Only God could have redeemed such a lost soul. He took a woman who by rights should have ended up in prison, an asylum, or the cemetery, and gave me a family, a purpose, and a law degree.

By God's grace, I'm able to serve in several ministry roles today, reaching out to young people who are having a hard time, like I did when I was growing up. My husband Peter and I visit Juvenile Hall every week, and it has proven to be a great ministry of love. We bring donuts and use the Foothills testimonial book *Kids Like Us* as a tool to reach into the lives of the children. For five years now, we have been able to share the gospel and the love of Jesus with the children and staff. God has used the healing that He did in me to help heal others, and that's an incredible thing to watch for someone who never thought she would be good for anything. But God certainly had a plan.

My life is a walking miracle. I have learned how a life of prayer can bring a hopeless, loveless child into a place of God's wonder and grace, and how God loves us so dearly. Even from the darkest, humblest beginnings, God can reach down and adopt us as His own.

Today I want everyone to know that no matter what hardships you may have in life, God can transform everything. He can change your heart and teach you to love instead of being scared, hurt, and angry. How do I know?

He redeemed me!

Kyle Hall

"What Prodigals Do"

It wasn't the first time I'd run away.

The first time was in high school. I fell in love with this girl, and she was a bad influence on me. I wasn't in a place where I cared much about that. Despite having been raised in the church and attending a Christian school, I started smoking pot, drinking a little, and getting deeper into a relationship with this girl.

Then we broke up, and it was like my world exploded.

It was a messy breakup. Shortly after, I crashed my motorcycle and broke my collar bone – and in the hospital I had my first experience with a drug other than marijuana. Already in a low place, I found that I liked the high I could get from harder drugs. It wasn't long before I dropped out of school and ran away from home.

I wasn't sure where my life was going. I partied as much as I could. That led to new drugs, and new problems. I made one real attempt to clean up my act, but that didn't last very long. Soon, I was right back in my addictions, and hanging out with the wrong crowd. A couple of years passed like this, just getting deeper into sin.

I remember at one point, I was driving around with some girls who had stolen drugs from somebody. I was in the passenger seat as we pulled into a gas station, and I didn't think there were any problems. I was laughing and joking when my door suddenly opened and some guy said, "Hey Kyle!" I turned to look at him, only to see a pair of brass knuckles heading for my nose. I got beaten up pretty badly as my friends laughed. There was blood running down my face when I finally managed to get out of the car and run into the gas station's convenience store. Someone called the cops, and I ended up standing in front of a sheriff's deputy, who asked me where I wanted to go.

And I didn't know.

The people I thought were my friends had betrayed me. They thought it was funny to set me up and watch me get beaten. I'd walked away from church and family a long time ago. I didn't know where to go.

"Come on," he said. "I've got to take you someplace."

At a loss, I gave him my parents' address. I'm sure it wasn't a reassuring sight for my mom to open the door and see me getting out of a squad car, all messed up. Mom took me in and cleaned off my face, and then my dad told me, "You know you can't stay here."

We just had no relationship at that point. I was deep in my addictions, we hadn't talked in a long time, and so I went out the door. They drove me to the hotel where I had been staying, and the next day, I got in my car and drove across the country.

As I was driving, I just felt so rejected. I felt isolated, without any friends or family. I was so ashamed of myself, like there was no hope. I had fallen too far from what I was supposed to be, and I didn't know what I was supposed to do now. I had never stopped believing in God, but He was the furthest thing from my mind. I didn't think He could forgive me and set me on my feet again. I certainly wasn't following Him.

So I did what prodigals do, and I ran away – for the second time.

I knew of a family friend in Florida who had a moving company, so I figured I might find open arms there. I got a job as a mover, and I made another attempt to live better. I still smoked a lot of weed and drank a lot – we'd go to the bars with the boys and drink at the house with the crew. I was that weekend warrior type, but every evening was the weekend, you know? I wasn't doing cocaine and stuff like I had been doing in San Diego, so on the outside it might have seemed like I was making a change, but in my heart I really wasn't. I was still broken. That nagging feeling that nothing makes any sense and that no one cares was getting worse and worse.

I found myself in my car on a Sunday night, alone, and I was freaking out. I tried to think of who I could call who would want to know what I was going through, but I couldn't think of a single person. The only one I knew for sure who would take that call was the family friend who would just help me get drunk again. I was trapped in a box, and it was like there was no way out. I was in despair, and the thought came to me that suicide was the only escape.

I cried out to God. I said, "God, if You're real, I need You to show me now!" And just like that, the Lord's presence filled the car.

It was like being wrapped in a big, warm hug. I felt the Lord say to me, "Kyle, I'm here. I'm real. I love you. I have a purpose for you."

My whole demeanor changed. In an instant, I had hope for life again. I got on my phone and searched for a church where I could go. I found a young adult group that was meeting, so I drove over and walked in, knowing nobody, just wanting to get where God was. They were in the middle of worship, and the song "Came to My Rescue" was playing. I remembered it from when I was a kid in church, and as I listened to the words, I was amazed.

I called, You answered
And You came to my rescue
And I want to be where You are

It was true! I had called at the depth of my need, and God had answered me. It was like confirmation that everything was going to be okay. I fell to my knees and recommitted my life to Christ that night.

I got involved at the church, and I had a strong desire to return home, but it was like the Lord kept telling me, "Not yet. You aren't ready." I talked to the leaders I met and the mentors at the church that took me under their wings, and they said the same thing. I had a lot of bad memories and bad influences back in San Diego, and I needed to heal first.

Being back in church was so refreshing. They eventually asked me to come work in the media department, and that meant I could quit the moving job where the guys wanted to take me drinking all the time. The Lord was patient with me, healed me from my addictions, and when the time finally came to return to San Diego, I came back the right way.

It wasn't the first time I'd run away, but it was the first time I'd ever really come home.

Greg Goodrich

"How Will I Make My Living?"

Turns out those "Caution, Wet Floor" signs are pretty handy.

My wife and I were at a sushi restaurant with Hank and Vicki Dmochowski in 2018, when things took a turn for the worse – and by things, I mean my knee. I'd gone into the bathroom, and the tile was slick. One wrong step twisted my leg 90 degrees to the side, and I fell.

There was no "Wet Floor" sign.

I was in agony – couldn't even stand up. I had to drag myself to my feet and get help out of the restaurant. It was terrible, but even worse was what I knew was coming as a result. You see, I've worked with my hands my whole life. I install rain gutters for a living, and that requires climbing around on your hands and knees up on a roof all day. With the kind of pain I was experiencing in my knee, I knew that wasn't going to be possible now.

I had limited health insurance, which complicated things. Going to the doctor would have cost an arm and a leg, and so I went to a chiropractor that I really trust to check out my injury. I paid for a round of laser treatments, and the chiropractor told me, "Seems like you tore an interior ligament. Yeah, your leg is out of place."

No kidding.

There wasn't much he could do for me, and what he could do didn't help all that much. He told me to call the restaurant to get them to pay for an MRI and all of that, so I did. They didn't call me back, though. I kept calling; they kept dodging. Short of a lawsuit, I was out of luck.

The reality was that I needed to be up on the roof to keep making a living for my family, so for the next three months I dragged my sorry self up a ladder every day and endured excruciating pain. My knee would dislocate a lot, and then I'd have to pop it back into place. I had to turn down a bunch of work because there was only so much that I could handle. I couldn't sleep at night. I'd toss and turn, and my wife was worried sick – both for my wellbeing and for our finances if I couldn't work.

I went forward at weekend services over and over to get prayer, but nothing happened. No improvement. I began to get discouraged. I remember thinking, "Come on, God! I need this for my work." It had me shaken up, and I stopped trying to get prayer for a while.

Finally, 3 months into the injury, I went to a worship and ministry service that Marc Dupont was leading at Foothills. Marc called for everyone with injuries to line the aisles, and so I limped to the aisle, literally popping my knee back into place several times. A young man in our church named Daniel Luckett came up to pray for me. He really took the time to understand what was going on and to wait on God in prayer, which I thought was neat. It was apparent that he was intent on seeing the Lord move in my situation.

He prayed for me, asked if there was any improvement, and there wasn't, but he didn't give up. He prayed again. We spent about ten or fifteen minutes this way – waiting on God, praying, testing, then starting over again. Finally, something was different after he prayed. My knee didn't hurt as much as before. I could move it a little better. I was excited as it continued to improve, and we prayed one last time together. "Lord, you're working. Please continue to work."

As I left and started walking to the car, I could feel it getting stronger. It was just improving more and more.

The next day, I went up to that first ladder and shot right up it. No pain at all. I felt like a million bucks! Work was easy that day, and I was rejoicing the whole time at this healing that God had done in me. Three months of terrible pain, and in one day it was good as new.

I'm 62 years old now, and I still climb up onto

roofs. My knee is healed from that devastating injury, and it's all thanks to the kindness of God.

Dr. Brian Lenzkes

"That Word Was for Me"

I didn't particularly want to speak up, but I think the Lord had other plans…

We were down in Guatemala on a medical mission trip through Foothills. There is a lot of need in that country, especially among the disabled and poor, so we go with a team of doctors and nurses to run a short-term medical clinic. We hand out medications, vitamins, reading glasses, and diagnose illnesses. We want to help the people live healthier lives, but we also know that God always opens doors for us to proclaim the gospel.

It's funny – we'll see these big, tough guys come into the clinic for the services we're offering, and when the subject of the Lord comes up, they're totally closed off because they don't want to submit to Him. Then, something happens, and the Holy Spirit moves to break down the walls of pride, and we see these same guys on their knees, crying out to Jesus. God gives us eyes to see all different kinds of pain when we're there, and Jesus is ultimately the remedy.

It's pretty amazing to see.

So on one occasion, we were invited to come and speak at a local church near our temporary clinic. Carlos Merlo confidently preached the Word, and it was powerful. You got the sense that people were really listening. As Carlos spoke, I felt like I got a word from the Lord for the congregation.

I felt a little uncomfortable. I'm not the type of guy who likes to run onstage and grab the microphone, so I thought, "I'm not going to just stand up and say something. I mean, if the opportunity comes, sure, but –" And then, at the front of the church, Carlos says, "Brian, do you have a word for the congregation?"

I could see I didn't have much choice then. I stood up and gave the word to the people.

It was about some of the men in the church being angry, drinking too much, and then coming home. They didn't have respect in their own houses because of their behavior. So it was this backwards situation, where these men were respected at work, but their homes were just in turmoil. I just spoke what the Lord placed on my heart about all of this, talking about alcohol abuse, abuse of the family, and what God desires for us. It must have been from the Lord, because it really spoke to the congregation.

When I was done, I remember this one guy got right up on his feet and made a beeline down the aisle toward me. Frankly, it was a little intimidating, because his jaw was set and he was a big, lumbering guy – but he just crashed into me to hug me. His knees buckled and I actually had to hold him up as he began to weep, and he told me, "That word was for me."

And he wasn't the only one. Right after him the next guy came up and said, "That word was for me."

Several members of our medical mission team had words of wisdom for individuals then, and it really felt like the Holy Spirit was present in a powerful way. The ministry was incredible, and I thought, "Maybe that's just how it is down here. Maybe they're just a very charismatic church."

Carlos, as usual, had to find out. He went to the pastor and asked him if it was like this every week, and the pastor said, "I've been doing this for forty-five years, and I've never seen anything like this." It gave us goosebumps, and we had to say that Jesus was passing by. We were seeing real changes in families and in individual lives.

We feel very blessed because we get to return year after year and see the fruit of this ministry – and it wasn't just a fluke! God really did intervene and change lives.

When I think back on this, I just have a strong impression of God's faithfulness when we step out to do His will. Even though I wasn't necessarily at the height of enthusiasm to speak, God gave me a word and made sure that I gave it, because He loves His people. It truly is a blessing to be used by God and see the good gifts that He pours out on His children.

Dustin and Jasmine McIntyre

"God's Heavenly Shore"

I'm going to warn you upfront, this is not a story of how our little boy was healed of cancer. We live in a world that is broken and fallen, and sometimes people die. Sometimes kids get sick. But even in the brokenness, God is still working for good. Even in hardship, maybe especially in hardship, God can mold our character and remind us that we're living for eternity.

This is a story of God doing just that.

We were the proud parents of three super healthy kids, but in October of 2011, we found out that something was definitely wrong with our son, Monty.

He had moments where he was very clumsy, like falling over. Then the symptoms turned to periodic vomiting. It would continue, then stop for a few weeks at a time, so we would just chalk it up to him being sick.

But then he threw up 11 times in one morning.

We took him to Children's Hospital where they gave him a CAT scan. I could tell by the nurse's reaction that there was something, that it wasn't good news.

They told me our son had swelling on the brain, likely a brain tumor, and they were going to admit him right then.

I never in my worst nightmare would have expected a call like the one I got from my wife that day. The nurses were kind of stunned by what they found. He had something attached to his brain the size of a golf ball.

Within a 24-hour period, we found out that it was very likely a malignant tumor, and his life expectancy was going to be… much shorter. And he was going to have a long road of chemotherapy and cancer treatment ahead of him.

I can remember very early on – probably the first day in the hospital – where we decided, "You know what? We're not going to curse God through this. We're going to trust in Him, and we're going to pray our way through this, but in the end He's going to be the peace that we lean on. And that's all we're going to need."

After Monty's very last round of chemo, the full dose of everything, we found out the cancer had returned. And that was very bad news, because that meant that now he needed his entire brain and spine radiated – which meant brain damage because he was so young. This was the point when we really started dealing with being devastated, with trusting in the Lord in this really hard, disappointing time. You know, like, "Why won't You answer our prayer?" and "What else can I do?" So, even then, we chose to trust God with our broken hearts. And He still really was there, genuinely giving a peace that does pass all understanding.

So ten months into treatment, we were given the worst news, and that was Monty's disease had gone widespread throughout his entire brain and spinal column and that... there wasn't a next step for treatment. They told us he would likely have weeks to a very few months to live.

Even through finding that out, that our long fight for Monty's life was at an end – now we get to enjoy him for the time we have left. Even though it was so hard, and you would think that you'd just want to be upset all the time, we chose to enjoy him. We chose to enjoy each other. And some of our best memories of our life are there, all crunched into that little time. I'll never forget that we could actually laugh, that we actually had God's joy, His presence, and just these sweet, good moments. Even in the midst of so much sorrow, there was really God's help and joy in those days. He never, never left us.

I think there was actually a lot of peace, or relief, when our son did pass, knowing that he's in a better place, knowing that he's fully cured and running around and jumping higher than he ever has before. I think that heaven became more real when our son passed away. We talk about heaven a lot more often. My daughter and I have a bluegrass project together, and a lot of the songs that we do are about heaven. It's just a reality to us that we will meet again on God's heavenly shore.

What you just read is a transcript of a testimony we wrote a few years ago, but we thought it was important to add a couple of things about the years since Monty passed away. The Lord gave us dreams and visions that helped us to mourn and gain closure. He gave us hope. He blessed us with three more children that we love and adore. We've seen the faithfulness of God again and again, and we know our Lord is compassionate. He was with us through the trial, and He met us on the other side.

Jhenifer Campos

"Pregnant With Tumors"

Pregnancy is difficult enough as it is – without complications.

In January 2014, I found out I was pregnant with a son, who would be our first child. We were excited and nervous like any first-time parents would be, and I was sure to schedule my checkups to keep an eye on things as the pregnancy progressed. Well, in March, during an ultrasound, the doctors found a 2.5cm fibroid. I was told not to worry about it. I sure didn't know that people were walking around with fibroids while pregnant, but they said it was normal, just to keep in mind that it would probably double in size before I gave birth.

I didn't think much of it, then. Life went on, and the baby inside of me grew.

In the beginning of my third trimester, the doctors and nurses kept asking me if I was in pain, because I'd gotten so big – my fibroid had swelled a lot, which didn't help, but I felt fine. I was still working 60 hours a week, and they said it wasn't dangerous. When I delivered my son, my fibroid was 13.5cm – about 5.5 inches, so it had looked like I was pregnant with twins. My son was 7lbs, 7 ounces, and pretty healthy.

My OB said not to worry about the fibroid, that it should shrink when my blood volume decreased post-pregnancy.

Two years later, I found out I was pregnant again. At a checkup in May, my OB told me I had not one but two fibroids – the original one that had gone down to 7cm and stayed that way, and the other was 2.5cm. They said it might double during pregnancy, and I was nervous because they had said that last time, and now I had two of them.

In July, I was told that my first fibroid had calcified, so it was a stone. It was like walking around with a rock in my stomach, and my second fibroid was 4 cm. When I delivered my daughter, my second fibroid had grown to 7.5cm.

I had my daughter, and the doctor said we should talk about removing the fibroids three months postpartum to give me time to heal. "Maybe it will shrink," she said, but there was no real hope for the one that had calcified. I was going to have to live with that unless they surgically removed it.

I went back to visit the OB again a few months later, and she suggested I get the fibroids removed if they were giving me problems. They said more than likely I would need a hysterectomy where they remove the uterus instead of just a myomectomy (which is just to get rid of the fibroids) because they were on the uterine wall. She recommended this anyway because the procedure would make me high risk if I were to have another pregnancy.

So if the fibroids were causing me pain, that would be it for having kids.

And the trouble was, I was in pain. My back was killing me, and I knew it was from the fibroids. So I was stressed out still from having a baby, a new-born, and now there was this, too. Unfortunately, this wasn't the end of our medical crises, either. On top of it all, my son had a submucous cleft palate and would need serious surgery and constant care as he recovered.

So I told the OB we'd have to talk about the hysterectomy later because of my son's upcoming surgery.

I put it off for about a year, and then at the beginning of 2018 I had really bad back pain, so my doctor said I should remove the fibroids.

I agreed that it was the fibroids causing me pain, but it was difficult because we weren't sure if we were done having kids. At the same time, I was tired of being in pain. I was undecided and neither solution sounded good, so I put it off a couple more months.

My son was having his surgery on May 4th, so the OB scheduled my surgery for August as long as my son's went well. I wouldn't be able to have any more kids, but at least my back would hopefully stop hurting all of the time.

I had started going to Drew and Lauren Miles' home group sometime in 2017, and I really loved it. I had tended to avoid home groups before that because my son is really hands on, and I figured that people don't always like it when the kids are in there with you. But the people at this home group really helped us out and accepted us, and we felt at home there. I got to talk about my marriage, my kids, and life. They would ask me if I needed prayer and I would tell them that my husband was stressed out at work, that my son needed to get his palate fixed, etc. Well, in August 2018, they asked me what they could pray about for me – and I said I didn't know. My marriage was good, my husband was content with his job, my son's surgery had gone well. I thought, "Things are good."

I remembered, suddenly, that I was going to get my pre-op MRI the next week, so I told them, "Well, I guess you could pray for me. I have a surgery." Everyone in the home group said, "What? You've never brought that up before, why not?" They were really shocked. I said, "I don't know, I don't really pray for myself."

Well, they weren't going to leave that alone. Six women laid their hands on my stomach and everyone prayed that God would heal me. I was super thankful, but honestly, I was thinking, "What is this going to do? I've had these for years. They're not cancerous." I was thankful for the women praying, but it was odd to me. I thought, "One of these fibroids is a stone. It's not going anywhere." I still prayed along with them, but I felt a little guilty.

The next week I got my MRI and they told me my calcified fibroid was completely gone and the other had shrunk to 4cm. So I went back to my OB, who asked me if I still wanted to have the surgery, and I said, "No!" I already got rid of the one I thought was never going anywhere. Maybe God would take the other one away too.

I cry a lot when I talk about this still because these fibroids and that surgery were a mountain for me. I'd had this problem for years – how could someone pray for healing and it's just gone?

So now here we are in September 2019, and I'm pregnant with our third child, and there are no fibroids. My son is now in kindergarten, and he's doing well. My daughter is healthy and happy.

I'm so thankful for our home group because I had felt alone before. I didn't have any family out here in San Diego, but the church and specifically our home group filled that need. It helped me hold on to my marriage and feel hope in the hard times. And I know that the prayer was why I was healed.

I don't have any fibroids! I keep asking every time I have an ultrasound, and they keep saying no. It's crazy.

We're naming our newest son Raphael. It means, "God has healed."

Jim Craig

"100% Disabled"

My back surgery went horribly wrong.

It all started with an industrial accident at work, and long story short, my back got injured. It was bad enough that I needed a laminectomy, but this is a minor surgery as far as back procedures go, so I wasn't too worried. The plan was to go into my back and take out a piece of bone from the injured disk to relieve the pain and pressure that I was experiencing.

During the operation, however, the doctor made a terrible mistake. He operated on the wrong disk and severed my spinal cord most of the way through. We assume what happened next was him trying to cover his mistake, because he sewed up the wound with sutures while I was still bleeding inside. A blood clot formed which crushed the remaining portion of my spinal cord.

I knew almost as soon as I woke up from the surgery that something was wrong. I couldn't feel my feet. I couldn't feel my legs. I knew that I had lost control from the waist down.

Aside from the paralysis, I was in excruciating pain. It was a disaster, and just like that, my life was dramatically changed. It took weeks before I could manage any movement at all, and that was just my big toe. I could wiggle it one-eighth of an inch.

I didn't get better. I didn't have a slow progression towards feeling coming back. My spinal cord was in two pieces, and the prognosis was that I would spend the rest of my life in a wheelchair. Working, lifting up my young daughter, going up a flight of stairs, and even walking down the street were all out of the question.

Using my upper hip muscles, which were the only part that really still worked, I eventually taught myself to sort of shuffle using a walker, but it wasn't practical. I had to use the chair. I was never going to have a normal life again.

I had been in a wheelchair for three years when Pastor Marc Dupont let me know about a prayer service that was going to be held at Foothills, and he suggested that I attend. My son Zach drove me to the service, and we sat in the front row. Marc came down immediately to say hi before things got going, and he brought the pastors and elders over to come pray for me.

To my mind, nothing was really happening, but I didn't know that God had already started a work.

Marc and the others left, going off to pray for others, and I remained in my spot. Now, I'm very careful not to use any "lightning bolt from heaven" language, but after three and one-half years of not feeling my legs, what I experienced was strange, to say the least. It was a bizarre feeling because my legs were so atrophied that they were pretty withered up and useless.

I leaned over and said to Zach, "I can feel strength in my legs." They were still numb, but I could feel strength in them. After a few more seconds, I said, "Zach, I think I can stand up." He said, "Dad, let me help you," and I told him, "I don't think I need any help."

Now, even if you sit down in a movie theater for two hours, you're a little wobbly when you stand up. That night I stood up out of my wheelchair, and I wasn't wobbly. I was sturdy on my legs.

I said to my son, "I think I can walk, but don't draw any attention to me." I left the wheelchair right there in the front row and walked around the church two times, no walker, no nothing. On the second time around, Marc and others saw that I was walking. They all came over and wanted to know what was happening, but I was in as much bewilderment as they were, because I knew the severity of my issues.

My wife wasn't there that night, so my son and I drove home after the service, and my wife and daughter came running out the door to see us – and there I was pushing my wheelchair up the driveway. She was literally in awe. Megan, my sweet daughter, came running to me, and I picked her up off the ground and held her like I hadn't been able to for the last three and one-half years. It was the best hug a father could ever get.

This was all so new and exciting for us – I didn't know where it was going to end or begin. Megan and I just took off and ran up and down the street in the middle of the night.

The doctors did an exhaustive round of tests on me after all of this happened. It was one doctor after another until they sent me up to Los Angeles to see three specialists. After being examined, all three came away with the same conclusion: Jim Craig is 100% disabled, the injury to his spinal cord is non-repairable, and he has 98% loss of feeling from the waist down. Three different neurologists told me this while I stood there in front of them on sturdy legs.

Two out of the three of them openly admitted that it was a miracle, that they'd never seen anything like this healing. My spine is in two pieces. Medically, it doesn't make sense that my legs work.

This was years ago, now, and today I'm still healed. I can go to Balboa Park and walk around, stand in front of exhibits, and exercise. I have full function of my legs.

I still have the MRI's, the document signed by doctors and sealed by a federal judge saying I'm

100% disabled. I show these to people. If anyone doubts that God is real or that He heals – my name is Jim Craig, and I'm a living, breathing, walking testimony.

It's a miracle! God is so good.

John West

"The Worst Pain in the World"

I've had back problems since my early twenties, and it just got worse the older I got. I worked in the shipyards, I was involved in martial arts – just about anything you can imagine, I did.

Pain was a central feature of my life. At least twice a year my back would go out. It got to the point where I had a major surgery. It helped, but the doctor warned me, "You've got two destroyed disks, and you've got to fix that." The only trouble is, death was a possible side effect of the surgery, so I decided not to do it.

Well, five years later, I was back.

They went in both sides, put in metal rods, and it took care of some of the problem – but I still had the pain. I've had a total of three spinal surgeries: one on my neck and two on my back.

I lived through pain management. The pain was affecting me emotionally, spiritually, and in every way. When my back would seize up on me, I'd end up on the ground. When it would slide out of place it was so intense that I only had about twenty minutes to get to a doctor to get a shot to relax my body. If I didn't get there in time, spasms would start. When you go into spasms and your back is out of place, it's the worst pain in the world. Forget about crying, I just wanted to die. It was terrible.

The pain was so constant and so intense that I became addicted to painkillers. I had to go on disability. It defined my life, in many ways.

It all got to be too much to bear, and one day while I was sitting at home griping to my wife, she told me, "Why don't you go to the healing center at church?" So I did.

At the healing center, they laid hands on me, anointed me with oil, and prayed for me. I felt the Spirit of God come upon me in a way that I don't think I've ever felt before. I could feel the pain leaving me right then, and I knew I was healed.

I was so confident that I was healed, that I flushed my medication down the toilet.

It's going on ten years now, and I haven't had so much as an aspirin. It's only because of what God did. He had mercy on me, and my pain is gone.

Right after getting healed I started walking. After a few weeks I started getting up into the hills. Now, I walk three or four miles a day every morning just spending time with Jesus and enjoying the beauty of His creation.

Kenny Delozier

"Jesus Healed Me"

I was out on disability for six months.

I haul fuel for a living, and I had fallen backwards out of a big rig truck and broken my wrist, but that wasn't the real problem. The fall messed up my C5 and C6 disks in my neck. The disks weren't lining up again how they were supposed to, and it was incredibly painful. I couldn't work. I went to the doctor for three months, and it didn't get better, so they sent me to a chiropractor for treatment. The chiropractor told me, "If we can't get this right, they'll have to operate on you." After three months, it still wasn't any better, so I had to go back to the doctor and schedule another appointment.

I really didn't want them to operate on my neck. There are always risks when you mess around with the spine, and sometimes things get worse after. But I was at the point where there wasn't really anything I could do.

Well, my wife was going to go to a prayer and ministry service at the church on a Wednesday night, and she asked me to go with her. I don't usually go to midweek events, but I felt the Holy Spirit tell me to go, so I went. At the service, Pastor Marc Dupont got up on the stage, and the second thing he said was, "Is there anyone here with problems with their C5 and C6 disks?" I ran down there and got prayer.

The next morning I woke up and I was normal. I told my wife, and she said, "You'll never be normal." And I said, "No, my neck feels good. It's healed like it was before the accident. It's normal." I told her, "I'm going to be nice to everybody today!" I was in a great mood and everything. So the next day I woke up, and it was still normal – and again the next day. Finally I went to the medical appointment they had scheduled for me, and I told the lady at the desk, "I'm here to cancel."

She said, "What do you mean? You've got a problem with your neck." I said, "No I don't. Jesus healed me." And I told the lady what had happened, and she looked at me like I was crazy. Even the doctor said, "This is hard to believe," but it's the truth, and I'm a walking testimony. I went back to work later that month.

I've never been back to the doctor since, and my neck is still normal and good. It's been almost a year and a half now.

Myrna Ames

"Small Steps of Faithfulness"

I came from a Christian background, but as an adult I was not following the Lord. A dear friend and coworker brought me to Foothills one Sunday, and I loved the worship part of the service. I wasn't onboard with the whole lifestyle, but I would come to listen to the music and to ease my conscience from time to time. I wasn't serious about listening to God's Word yet. It would take time, but the Lord began slowly softening my heart.

In the next season, I was convicted by the Word, and I promised God that I would attend church every Sunday and give a small tithe every month. I said, "Lord, You know me and how I'm not a faithful steward, but with Your help I can be faithful." So I came every Sunday morning and I tithed the amount I'd promised, and the Lord was with me.

Three months later, Mark Hoffman called for us to pray 15 minutes a day. He put a card in the bulletin to help us called "The Secret Place: An 8

Day Plan" which told us to pray in Thanksgiving, Praise and Worship, Soul Searching, and Requests. I wanted to dedicate my heart to prayer, and I gave my pledge again, asking for the Lord's faithfulness to be put in my heart – and again the Lord was with me.

The following summer I asked the Lord about giving 10% of my salary in tithe. I was afraid, once again not knowing if I would be able to be faithful. The Lord was with me, however, and I tithed 10%. As time went on, the Lord put it on my heart to contribute to Youth Venture, so I increased my giving. Then there was a need for a building expansion, and when I increased my giving that time it really cost me because my income was reduced at the same time, but the Lord was with me and helped me be faithful in stewarding my finances – an area I'd always struggled with.

The Lord was building my faith during all of this time, which was really tested once when I was in fear of losing my job. What had happened was my boss was doing some serious downsizing, and I took that to be an inevitable sign of layoffs. He had me sell off filing cabinets, desks, and wall units – my desk was the only thing left. I knew that it was only a matter of time before I would be fired, so I prayed every day and cried out to God to help me. After all, I had a daughter to put through college, and I was the one providing health insurance for my family. I just couldn't afford to lose my job.

One morning, I tried to say the Lord's Prayer to begin my devotions like I had every day for the previous four years – and I couldn't remember the words. I opened my mouth and nothing came out. I said, "Lord, I have no words and I'm so frightened that I'm going to lose my job." In my heart, it felt like the Lord asked me, "Do you trust Me?" "Of course I trust You! But I know how this works, the handwriting's on the wall and I'm going to lose my job!" Again, He seemed to ask me, "Do you trust Me?" Frustrated at having to repeat myself, I opened my mouth and stopped, suddenly realizing that I didn't really have all my trust in Him. I blurted out, "No, I don't trust You. I've prayed and prayed, and it seems like I'm the only one talking here. I don't see Your hand moving, and I don't even know if You exist! You never show Yourself to me, and I'm the only one talking all of the time!"

My hand shot to my mouth, horrified as I sank to the floor. I began apologizing to the Lord about my outburst. I got on my knees and tried to say the Lord's Prayer, and I still couldn't remember the words until eventually, they just came. After reciting the prayer and feeling His peace wash over me, I prayed, "I'm sorry that I said those things, Lord. I do believe You, and I lay all of this down at Your feet. I trust You for my job and my finances. I give it all to You and I know whatever happens, I'm in

Your hands. I'm letting this go."

Two weeks later, my boss called me into his office... but not to fire me. He had merged with another school, so all of the downsizing was to make room for their equipment. I had worried and walked around anxious for no good reason – but even then the Lord was faithful while I was throwing a fit. He was still with me, and He used the opportunity to draw me closer.

Another area where I had to learn to trust God was with my husband. For years I would come to church and save a seat for him, but he wouldn't come. I saved a seat for him every week anyway, deciding that I hadn't given up on my husband and I was going to trust God. Eventually, my husband did come to church. In time, he gave his life to the Lord, and today we have a wonderful Christian marriage. God was with me again.

Today, I'm finding that waiting on the Lord, praying for others, reading His Word, and seeking Him has brought me closer and closer to Him. If I want to be like Him, I need to love what He loves and hate what He hates. Reading Proverbs helps me recognize His attributes. The Psalms help me cry out to Him. And as we become more like Him, we will know Him better because we will see Him in each other.

These small steps of faithfulness, maybe unre-
markable when taken one by one, all add up to a
changed life, a heart of hope, and a future.

Robert Davila

"The Cancer Came Back"

I remember growing up in a Catholic home, but I didn't have much of a relationship with God until my parents sent me to a local Christian school. We would attend daily chapel, and my walk with the Lord began to change. I began to hear the voice of God and His plan for me. Eventually, I accepted Jesus into my heart and unknowingly started a life of serving and loving God's people. I was baptized and have walked this life of service for many years.

Then, in 2012 I was crushed in a backhoe accident. In the hospital, the doctors discovered I had metastatic thyroid cancer. How was I supposed to serve others now?

Besides, I was overwhelmed by fear. I was facing an operation in which there was a high chance I would lose my voice. My business, my life, centered around my ability to relate with people. How could I do the things I do without a voice? What would be the last words my wife and kids would hear me say? And as if that wasn't enough – Would I live through cancer?

One fear that haunted me was my family's financial future if I were not in the picture. How would they survive? In a quiet time, the Holy Spirit came to me in a soothing, captivating way. He told me I did not need to worry about the finances. He said the "money is nothing." He reminded me that I had taught my children well, and I had given them the skills to move through this life with the strength of character.

The surgery was successful, although there were several others to follow. I did not lose my voice. I found myself declaring, "Thank You, God!" There was a respite in which I was clear of cancer, and life was moving on. My intimacy with God grew stronger and more fulfilling. He gave me clear instructions on how I was to relate with His children. My heart is to bring people into the presence of God, and serving others in this time was such a joy.

Then, years later, cancer came back, and this time it was stage four.

In many ways, I felt like I was back to square one – back on the bench again and fearing for my life. The threat of more surgeries became real once more, and I became frustrated with the prospect of facing that pain. Frustrated, I considered suicide.

I confided what I was feeling to my best friend

Jeff. He is a man I can talk truth with and not feel judged. I thank God for his friendship. Jeff gave me a nugget of advice that paid dividends: He suggested I go to Foothills' healing center and let them pray for me. I reluctantly took his suggestion and made an appointment. At the center, two people prayed for me. They prayed that I would get healed, but they also suggested something I thought was crazy. They instructed me to begin a process of "feeling God's glory in everything." "How am I supposed to do that?" I wondered. "I have cancer, and I have gone through this hell over and over." Ultimately, I decided to follow their advice. After all, the Word of God says to do just that: "Consider it all joy, my brethren, when you encounter various trials" (James 1:2).

Here is the kicker. I had to get an ultrasound before the next surgery. In that process, the technician found nothing. My doctors looked at the results and could not believe what they saw. I was healed. No more cancer. To this day, I am cancer-free. My life was restored.

This is going to sound funny, but cancer was the best thing that ever happened to me. I am content with my life now. Whatever comes, God's got this. Before, I would grow frustrated when I couldn't fulfill my God-given purpose, but now I see that God is sovereign even in the times of hardship or in waiting. I used to fear what would become of the people I loved when I was no longer around to serve them, but I learned that God, in His great love and power, will look after His own.

I want people – my family, my friends, my employees, my customers, and every stranger I meet – to see God in me. I am learning how to give hope to others, not just through my story, but at a deeper, spiritual level. My desire is for them to know the love and strength of Jesus. My business has become a church, a place to meet Jesus Christ. This life is short, and eternity means so much more. Through the hardships I've endured, I have seen how precious every moment is. I have learned how to enjoy this life with great excitement and anticipation.

I am blessed – blessed to serve, blessed to wait, and blessed that God is in control of all things.

Roxanne Fulkerson

"God Healed My Painting Hand"

I should begin this testimony by telling you that I am a painter. It was always my dream to be a visual artist, and finally, these past years, that dream has come true. With finely controlled flicks of the wrist, visions and designs come to life on the canvas, and I love it.

Then something terrible happened.

In August of 2014, my husband and I were camping with our family in the Sierras. In the middle of the night, I needed to get up and use the campground restroom. On the way back to our camping spot, I stepped into a deep hole, fell, and shattered my left wrist. Having broken bones before, I instantly knew it was broken. Looking at my limp hand confirmed this. The pain was excruciating and nauseating, and it caused me to pass out. My son Wes caught me and laid me inside the camper. My husband went to get help and call an ambulance.

Being up in the Sierras was not the best scenario

for an ambulance. The nearest hospital was an hour away. After a painful waiting period, I was taken to the hospital and treated.

When we returned home several days later and I saw a specialist, they set my wrist and said it should heal without surgery. That was not the case. Two weeks later, upon looking at another x-ray, the doctor said the bones were not coming together but separating. Surgery was needed. What other choice did I have? I could hardly hold a paintbrush.

I went through with a procedure, in the hope and understanding that things would begin getting better. Unfortunately, after surgery the pain was off the charts. What should have been a 45-minute stint in recovery turned into a five-hour stay as they could not get the pain under control and did not know why. Then, during the rehabilitation process, a tendon snapped in my thumb. The thumb was already hanging limp and not responding to therapy. After further tests, it was discovered that a nerve and tendon had been pulled and partially ruptured. That was the reason for all of the pain. Had an MRI been done before surgery, the tendon could have been repaired. Now I was being told by yet another hand specialist that the only hope for even a possibility of using my thumb again was to borrow a tendon from another finger with unsure results.

I decided against more surgery. I continued in

rehab and kept praying that God would heal my unusable thumb.

In 2016, Foothills did a Sacred Assembly, which focused on repentance, forgiveness, and adoration for God. In preparation, we prayed and fasted. My husband Jeff and I are part of the prayer ministry, so when the day of the event came around, we met with the rest of the team before going out to pray for others. One of the pastors said someone had a word that people with metal in their wrists and or ankles were going to be healed. I knew in my spirit that was me. I also knew that I had committed to pray for others, so I felt that I could not answer the call to have someone pray over me.

I prayed for several people, and then there was a lull. I asked Pastor Jim Deyling who it was that had the word about healing. He said it was Shane Blafield, so I went to find him. Shane and two others prayed for me, and I got a tiny bit of movement in my thumb. They prayed again. I moved a tiny bit once more. They prayed again, and the same bit of movement was apparent.

That night on the way home, my husband and I were rejoicing at what it seemed that God was doing. I stayed up late just to praise God. All of a sudden, I remembered that I could not open my hand all of the way and had forgotten to mention that to Shane and the others. With trepidation, I turned my arms palms up, like in praise, and tried to open my hand. Glory to God – it opened all of the way!

Over the next weeks and months I continued to improve. The biggest miracle was that I could not only move my thumb, I could also do the hyper flex movement (like used in hitchhiking). There is no tendon there. That is the one that was ruptured and gone. I praise God that I have this testimony to show people. There is no tendon in my thumb, yet I am not hampered by the injury at all.

Sierah Palafox

"A Broken Person"

Let me tell you, over fifteen years of sustained, severe back pain is no picnic.

I herniated a disc while playing soccer in 2006, and a few months later I was in a major car accident, which made the pain worse. I was diagnosed after the accident with degenerative disc disease at the age of 16.

At only 17 years old, I had to have back surgery. I recovered well, or so I thought, and had a good year afterward. But my degenerative disc disease caused my back to get worse, and so I was prescribed nerve medication to help with the intense sciatic pain I began to experience. The physical and emotional pain was so unbearable. I couldn't imagine living my whole life this way.

At the age of 18, I had given up on trying to deal with being a "broken" person, and I tried to take my life. I poured out a mess of pills, swallowed, and told God that if I woke up, I knew He had a purpose for me and I would keep going.

To my own surprise, I woke up. I figured that meant that I did have a purpose, but I still didn't know how to live with this pain.

Over the next ten years I went on to try different medications and treatments, and I received semi-annual epidurals of steroid injections. Some things worked for a while; other treatments made no difference. I had an absurd number of medications to take every day, but at times my pain would be so severe that I had to walk with a cane or walker, or was unable to walk at all. As a result, I lost three different jobs.

I was serving in youth ministry during these painful years. I have a passion for the youth, and I wanted to help as much as I could. But even in ministry, I was limited physically and unable to serve the way I wanted to.

In 2017, I crashed. I was being tapered off of a nerve medication that also doubled as an antidepressant. Until this time I had never been diagnosed with depression, because I was unknowingly treating it with the medication. As I was weaned off of nerve medications, I felt the full emotional and mental weight of my condition and the depression it caused. I stayed in my room and cried for three weeks, not understanding why I felt so low. I started meeting with a Christian counselor here at Foothills.

In the same year, I saw a surgeon about an implant in my back to help block some of the nerve pain through electronic pulses. Some patients have success with it, so I was willing to go through with the surgery to give it a try. After reviewing my history, he decided I wasn't a candidate for the operation. If other treatments were unsuccessful, this would be too. As discouraging as that news was, I had a spark of hope that God could heal me. At this point, it was my only option.

In January 2018, I was scheduled for another epidural, but I had a sense that I should not do it. I canceled the appointment and decided to wait for the Lord to show me what I should do.

Around that same time, I started serving in the high school ministry here at Foothills and I got to know Alison Bennett. I came limping into a Saturday night service in July 2018 when Alison saw me walking in with my cane. She pulled me aside at the end of the service and prayed for me.

She didn't actually pray for my back to be healed, but for my mental state and to be able to do youth ministry. That was pretty much all she prayed. Sciatica or any other type of nerve pain can take a huge toll mentally, because the suffering is constant and you can't do anything to stop it. Alison prayed for that mental struggle, not my back pain itself.

That night as I left the service, I felt a little better but I was still in pain. So you can imagine how surprised I was when I woke up in the morning and realized I had slept through the entire night. I hadn't gotten a full night's sleep in years. When I woke up in the morning, I texted Alison to say thanks for her faithfulness. She said she would continue to pray.

Over the next few months, I continued to monitor my pain and would test my back to see if I was getting better. I would try doing things I could never do before and slowly started to taper off all of my pain and nerve medications. Within three months, I was completely off of my meds and pain free.

I didn't realize how much my physical pain impacted every part of my life, until I had to learn how to live normally over the next several months. I was gripped with the fear of throwing my back out, hesitant to commit to things, and not very active. Day by day, I had to learn how to function, develop new habits and accept my healing to finally live well.

It took six to eight months to learn how to not be broken - physically, mentally and emotionally. A lot of fear and doubts tried to creep in, causing me to question if I was really healed.

But the pain just didn't come back.

By October of 2018, I had lost 50 pounds. I was finally able to walk and move, so the weight came off relatively quickly and easily. I now feel better at 30 years old than I ever felt in my 20s.

Everything in my life has completely changed. I

am now serving as a youth leader at a church in La Mesa. This has been my dream and calling since I was 17. If I had been offered the job a year before, I would have turned it down; I wouldn't have been physically able to do the work.

Over the past year, I have seen people that I haven't seen in a long time and each of them have recognized immediately that I walk differently, much faster. It is so exciting to be able to tell everyone who notices that it was Jesus who healed me!

Chuck Hicks

"Can You Believe That Just Happened?!"

Quite a few years ago, my friend Tony and I were doing street ministry together. What we would do is take a wagon, put a bunch of baloney sandwiches and cans of soda in it, and reach out to street people with lunch and the gospel. We were just trying to be faithful in sharing the good news that God had given to us, and we figured that the snack wagon was a good way to show that we come in peace.

So one day, Tony and I were out making the rounds, and there was an old lady with one of those walker/baskets you push around. She was really unkempt, pretty obviously homeless. I went up to her to offer her some food, and we broke the ice with friendly conversation.

She was living on the street, she told us, and didn't have a job. She told us about all sorts of problems in her life, and it led to a point in conversation, where I said, "Have you sought the Lord in these things? Because He's a God who likes to answer prayers." She got mad then, and cussed a lot. Finally, at the climax of her tirade, she said, "God can't even feed my gosh dang cat." (full disclosure, she didn't say "gosh dang.")

So I said, "God is interested in every detail of your life. He wants a relationship with you that's real and personal and wants to walk alongside you and bring you through life. He wants to bless you."

She said, "I don't believe any of that. God can't even feed my gosh dang cat."

We had been walking as we talked, and just then we reached the corner of the sidewalk to see a '67 Toyota truck take a turn a little fast. Something fell out of the tailgate and rolled by us, so I took a step and picked up what had fallen. It was a can of Friskies cat food.

I gave it to the homeless lady and said, "This is such a small thing for God." I was wearing my poker face, very calm and quiet. Tony didn't say anything.

Well, this lady started saying, "Oh my God. Oh my God. There's just no way." She was amazed.

I told her "God's interested in every detail, He cares about your cat, He knows everything. Have you ever given Him a chance or trusted Him with your life?"

She said, "No, never gave God much thought."

"Why don't you let Him into your life and let Him lead you?" I said.

"How do I do that?"

This was a wide-open door to share now, so I told her the gospel. She had heard bits and pieces of it before but had never really considered it. At the end of it all, I asked her if she believed that Jesus died on the cross for her sins. She said, "I do now."

"Jesus wants to be a part of your life," I told her. "Are you willing to let Him?"

She said yes, and then we prayed over her, and she said she felt different. A bus she had been waiting for showed up, so she got on, which left Tony and I walking away in silence. But once we had rounded a corner, I let out a huge breath and began laughing, and Tony jumped up and down shouting, "I can't believe that just happened! Did you see that? The can fell right off the truck!"

We were in absolute disbelief at the sign God had sent to this woman. I'd never seen anything quite like that.

A few years later, on Main and Magnolia, I saw an old lady who was very well-dressed and well-kept. She must have seen me because she drove up in her car, parked, and walked over to introduce herself to me. Her name was Marge, and she said, "You don't remember me, but…" and then she told me all about the time two men with a wagon full of sandwiches told her about God.

She was living in a house with two other ladies, attending church, and she actually sang in the choir.

Her life had completely turned around, all because
of the gospel and a can of cat food.

AJ and Lauralee Guerrero

"He Saved Our Marriage"

AJ: I remember the first time I saw her. From that first moment, Lauralee caught my attention, and we quickly became friends and just kept pursuing that relationship.

Lauralee: We got married at 22.

AJ: I remember saying my vows and looking at her and thinking, "This is going to be the rest of my life, and that's a great thing."

Lauralee: Things were really good for a while. We had our daughter Kylie, we bought a house…

AJ: Money was just coming in, almost like it was too easy. I was in construction at the time and we were doing a lot of work. I still had plenty of time to spend with my family, and things were just going well until all of the sudden, construction hit an all-time low and there was no work. Owners were strapping on their tool bags to keep their families afloat, and guys like me were just out of luck. The slowdown lasted a long time, and we ended up having to foreclose on our house while Lauralee was pregnant with our second child.

Lauralee: So he would work from seven in the morning until like three, taking whatever work he could, come home and take a shower, then go to school from five to ten. He was trying to move into a culinary career since he had always been interested in it and construction was so inconsistent. So this was what life was like when our son Eric was born. I was by myself a lot, and I felt lonely, and I missed him.

AJ: I felt like I was doing everything I could for the family and not understanding Lauralee's side. That's when the arguments began, and I started withdrawing. I started pushing her in a way that I wanted to get away from her. Eventually we turned to each other, a year and a half down the road, and we realized we didn't even have a relationship anymore. It got to the point one day where I finally called and said, "I'm coming home, but I'm coming to get my stuff."

Lauralee: When I heard that, I was kind of like, I know that we're not happy, but I wasn't ready for that... to split up our kids. I was driving, and I asked him, "Are you serious? Is that really what you want to do?" And he said, "Yes." I got off the phone, and I was sitting there thinking, "What would that look like?" I had prayed before in my life – I think everybody prays sometimes – but I had never prayed and expected God to answer. So for the first time, I did. I said, "Ok, I don't know what to do. God, tell me what to do," and I expected an answer. And He did answer. He told me, "Could you imagine every day without AJ?" And I said, "No." He said, "Could you imagine sharing your kids, sending them off?" And I said, "No." So He told me, "Then don't do that." And I said, "I can't fix this, we can't talk to each other. How are we supposed to go on from here?" And He told me, "Just trust Me. I'll hold your hand and I'll show you."

I didn't know if I'd be able to change my husband's mind or get him to listen to me. He didn't want to. When he came in, he said, "I'll listen to you, but then I'm getting my stuff and I'm going." So I said, "Ok. Well, I want you to know that I'm sorry. And that I know you feel lonely, and I don't want to give up on our family." There was a visible change in his posture and in his eyes, and it felt like he actually started to listen to what I had to say.

AJ: I remember sitting there thinking, "How is she

sorry? How can she mean that right now, after all I've done to push her away? How is it possible that she's saying sorry to me?"

Lauralee: After that, we were still dealing with our same problems, but we were doing it in a better way, at least. Then one day I was doing dishes, and I just heard in my heart, "Go to church." And I thought, "Okay… What was that?" Then I heard it again: "Go to church." I called AJ at work and told him, "So we're gonna go to church," and he was like, "Why?" We hadn't been in… a long time, but he said yes and told me to pick a church to go to.

AJ: We went to Foothills a couple of times, and it felt great. The worship was awesome, and it made me feel good, but it wasn't until Easter when the story of the resurrection came out and I *felt* my sin on that cross. It was the first time I realized that Jesus, the one we call Savior, is my Savior and that He has a plan for us.

Once we gave our lives to Christ as husband and wife, we started to see all of the strongholds and all of the walls break down rapidly – all the things we thought we would have to deal with for a very long time or forever. They started breaking down, and it can't be explained other than by Christ.

Lauralee: He saved our marriage, and then He saved our souls.

AJ: In the five years since all this happened, God has blessed us so much. I don't want to come across like I'm preaching a prosperity gospel, but it's just true that the more we let God in and ask Him to guide us through our life decisions, the more the Lord has worked in a big way. Today, my life with my wife is something that I never even could have imagined before, and it's an unconditional kind of love. We've continued to grow, and our children all love the Lord and are such a joy.

I look at the path that my family was headed down when the Lord intervened, and I'm so thankful that God met us in the midst of that storm. He completely changed our family history for His glory.

Teri Bowen

"A Cure for the Pain"

My childhood seemed pretty normal from the outside: Educated parents with good careers, vacations, girl scouts, and pets. We even went to Catholic church, but I hadn't yet learned that God loves me. Everything seemed fine at a glance, but it wasn't.

I was a mess of unsorted feelings, the sort of anguish and passion that don't fit well into a small child – and I had desires that don't fit well into a small child either. As young as kindergarten I remember having the desire for sex. This became the silent obsession of my childhood, first as daydreaming and eventually as actual promiscuity. I found some *Playboy* magazines in a field by my house early on, and I used to look through them, thinking I wanted to be like those ladies when I grew up.

By the time I was nine or ten years old, my mess of emotions began bubbling to the surface. I cried every day, I worried constantly, and I just felt pain in my soul. I was out of control, and these feelings were constant. We weren't allowed to be joyful, happy kids in my house, and we certainly weren't allowed to cry or express any kind of emotions either, so I learned to stuff them down, hiding the inexplicable anger, hurt, and sadness that I felt at all times.

I had no ambition, no drive, no self-confidence, and no identity. I felt dead inside. I was tested for learning disabilities in school, but the reason I couldn't learn much was because I was so shut down.

The existential angst became so unbearable that I became suicidal. I wanted to die, and every night I had dreams of dying. When my dreams turned to depicting family members dying, I ran crying to my mother, who sent me to therapy.

When I was in fifth grade, my parents split up, and I was already drinking. They were too wrapped up in their own lives to notice the path I was heading down. At any rate, they didn't do anything to stop it. I began having sex soon after.

Then one day, when I was in the sixth grade, something happened that would alter the trajectory of my life. I went to youth group at a friend's church, and then I went on a retreat with them where I accepted the Lord. Everyone seemed so happy for me! They gave me a Bible, and there were all of these smiling, happy faces around. I do believe that this was the moment of my salvation, but I was very young, very broken, and I didn't understand all of the implications. I still had many years of destructive living ahead of me.

By the time I was in high school, I had been diagnosed with major depression. I didn't like myself and didn't understand why I was in so much pain. Life went on, and I sank further down.

I picked terrible friends and boyfriends. I got pregnant twice by one boyfriend who I was with for three and one-half years, but both babies are in heaven now. The first one was aborted, and I lost the second one during pregnancy, nearly dying of sepsis in the process. This boyfriend was emotionally abusive to me, convincing me that no one else would ever want me. When I lost the second baby, however, the emotional and verbal abuse turned physical. I was so deluded at the time that I thought I really loved him, but the violence was enough of a shock for me to realize that I needed to escape the toxic relationship.

I still had that emptiness, that pain, sorrow, and rage that I could not understand, and I tried to fill it with everything I could think of: More boyfriends, hippy culture, lots of alcohol, and then drugs. I started with pot, then moved onto speed and cocaine. If you can believe it, I actually felt superior to others just because I told myself I'd never do heroin. LSD became my drug of choice because it numbed my thoughts, numbed the pain, and numbed my existence. I could be out for eight hours at a time, which was my kind of coping.

This kept the pain away for a couple of years, but then it came back, and the drugs wouldn't do anything about it.

Church was on the periphery of my life a few times. I was briefly around the Jesus Movement but didn't stick with it. I tried a Presbyterian youth group for a while, but it didn't stick – or I didn't. After bouncing around from group to group looking for something I didn't quite understand, I started taking classes in something called "Psychic Development." I liked what I found there, and so I took more classes, went to seminars, séances, and hung out with these people. It took a lot longer for me to receive a spirit guide than the others in these classes, but eventually one came. In a class called "Transcendental Meditation," I learned how to see my spirit guide, and I could see him whether my eyes were open or closed. He looked beautiful.

If you've never heard of spirit guides or transcendental meditation before, understand that they are not God-honoring things. It's a very mystical and pagan type of practice, and, as I later came to understand, spirit guides are not the beautiful beings they present themselves as but are unclean spirits.

But I didn't know that yet. I meditated every

morning and night. I found a kind of peace, for a while.

Then my older sister found out what I was doing, and she started praying for me. She was a Bible-believer, and she was determined to pray me right out of the mystic circles I was running in. Thankfully, her prayers were answered, because the connections suddenly just failed. I couldn't communicate with the spirits anymore, so I got bored and dropped it.

I was still seeking a cure for the pain, however, so I decided to go with my mom to her church. I met with God again, and I got baptized and started to read the Bible. I felt hopeful for the first time in years.

I still had my demons to battle. Healing would take some time, but God had a hold of me, and He wasn't letting go, and I wasn't letting go of Him either. The drugs and the alcohol weren't hard to give up, but they were a crutch when something hard happened in my life. Same with the promiscuity. When I experienced setbacks, I'd fall into a cycle of sleeping around and all my old habits, but the difference was this time I had an idea that God loved me and didn't want these things for my life. I fell often, but I would always come to God on my knees in repentance, and he'd pick me up again.

I had a lot of confusion and was still sorting out how to feel about love. My years of promiscuity meant I was sick from the waist down for a long time, on and off of medications. STDs are a terrible thing to experience.

When I began to face the truth about myself, I realized that I first had to deal with all of the bad choices that I had made to cover up the pain. I needed to make things right with God before I could go deeper and find the source of this mysterious, lifelong agony. I still cried all the time, but I was seeking the Lord.

I began to really study the Word of God and understand it better, and a pastor named Michell Cook and his leadership team really took me under their wings. I underwent a yearlong process of deep inner-healing with two wonderful women. God was so faithful to reveal things to me that needed to be dealt with. He was cleansing me so that He would be glorified in my life and so I could feel His love.

I happened to tell someone at a church event about my spirit guide, and they weren't enthusiastic like I thought they would be. After all, one of my old mystic friends said that his spirit guide was Jesus, so I thought that there wasn't anything wrong with it. The people at church encouraged me to tell the spirit guide, "If you are not from the throne room of God, you have to leave." I told them that I would say that, but I assured them that this spirit guide was of God. It wasn't. When I said what they had told me to say, it left.

I had to do some serious unravelling of all the deception I had bought into during my mysticism phase. I was still meditating for a time and would sometimes see an odd manifestation, but again I said, "If you are not from the throne room of God, you have to leave," and it did.

My mother was on a journey of healing at the same time as I was, and she revealed to me the abortion she had done on herself before she married my father, and that she didn't want me when she found out that she was pregnant with me. It was heavy, the things that the Lord was walking me through, but it was good to find out the truth and forgive, and I began to have a transformed mind and emotions. I was able to own up to my errors and forgive those who had done me wrong.

But something wasn't right. I still had that deep, mysterious pain I'd had ever since I could remember. I still couldn't deal with the lust I felt. But God says, "You will seek Me and find me when you search for Me with all your heart" (Jeremiah 29:13), and that turned out to be true. I went to Bible studies, twelve-step programs, recovery groups, CODA, SA, Nor-Anon, but none of them seemed to strike at the issue directly. Then my counselor suggested I go to a sexual abuse survivor support group – and I found that these people spoke my language. During a year with this group, God revealed to me in a dream about the young man who had molested me when I was just an infant. He showed me his face so I could understand what had happened and forgive him. Then, I was finally able to move on.

This past May 2019, I celebrated 30 years of being faithfully married to my best friend. I've been able to stay faithful – and I never thought I'd be able to say that. God healed me in the deepest corners of my soul.

I'm free from my past. The old things have lost their grip, and I've fallen deeper in love with the One who loved me first. It's been a long and messy road, but God loved me enough to walk down it with me.

Jennifer Young

"I Don't Live in Despair Anymore"

The story of my old life comes down to two facts: I always wanted to be loved, and my mom didn't know how to do that.

I was raised in the Mormon Church, and I bounced between different homes – sometimes legally through CPS, and sometimes it was just my mom passing me around. Law enforcement would get involved from time to time. I was a foster kid with a verbally and physically abusive mom, so "home" was never a stable concept for me. And yet I really yearned for my mother's approval. I wanted her to care for me, to tell me that she was proud of me. I never got my wish.

As a result, I was very depressed. Life didn't seem worth living, so by the time I was 16 I told my mom that I was ready to kill myself. Mom's response was, "Okay. Just call your therapist one more time before you do."

How hard is it to say, "Hey, please don't kill

yourself" or, "I love you" when your daughter says what I said?

Not sure what else to do, I did call my therapist, and he had me come into the mental hospital. It was the first time I'd been admitted for thoughts of suicide. After they released me, I didn't go back home to my mom for the next two years.

I tried to reconnect with my mom one last time when I was 18 years old. I came home again, but it was all the same. Abusive, cold, critical. So, feeling like I would never be accepted or loved, I tried to take my own life.

It was an overdose. As I was fading away, I kept calling out for my mom, who was just in the next room, but she wouldn't answer. At one point, I managed to crawl out to where she was, but she still refused to acknowledge me. Unable to stand and at the end of my consciousness, I crawled back into my room and prayed, "God, if You're real I'm coming to You now, because I can't take this anymore." I began stabbing myself then, and I blacked out.

I lived. I wouldn't have without the paramedics taking me to the hospital. My mother must have called them, but when I saw her, all she would do was laugh at me for swallowing pills and stabbing myself. She said I was an idiot and should have just picked one method. She told me that I managed to mess up something so simple as suicide.

The truth is, I was on a razor's edge between life

and death, and they had to perform open heart surgery on me to pull me through.

Apparently my mother called my father at some point to tell him what had happened, and he called his Christian ex-wife, and she called her church – and the church sent a pastor to come pray for me in the ICU. He prayed that I would receive salvation and that God would spare my life. Despite not knowing this man personally, it gave me hope to see the care and concern he had for my life.

I didn't have anywhere to go after I was discharged, so this pastor and his family invited me to stay with them. His wife said that God had put it on her heart to open their home to me, so I lived with them for three and a half months, and it was a healing and revealing time.

See, when I was twelve, my mom's Christian hairdresser invited us to church. Being Mormon, we were taught that we *were* Christians – just the kind that know a little more. So we didn't think it would be all that different, but once we got into the service, I was in awe of this Jesus that they preached. I had never heard that Jesus loves me. On my one, single visit to a real church, I went forward to get saved, and I believe this is the day that I became a real Christian. I cried and cried. In retrospect, that moment probably kept me from attempting suicide a lot earlier.

But after that one Sunday, I stayed in the

Mormon Church because I was twelve and didn't know the difference. Nothing was the same after that day, but I couldn't quite put my finger on it. It was like my eyes were opened.

In the Mormon Church, young girls stand in for the dead in ritual baptisms. (If that sounds weird and unbiblical, that's because it is.) The woman who led the rites would always ask us, "Don't you feel great! You feel good, right?" And everyone would say, "Yes," because we were brainwashed, but I didn't feel good, and I'd say so. Every time I participated in baptisms for the dead I'd get a splitting headache. I'd sneak Advil and give some to the other girls just to get through it.

All this is to say that theologically and doctrinally, I was really lost, without a leg to stand on. That day in the ICU, that prayer of salvation was a recommitment in my heart, and living in the pastor's house was the first time I was ever discipled and instructed in Jesus' teachings. It was a lot of unravelling. A lot of undoing the lies of the Mormon Church, asking questions, and learning from the Bible.

So, after leaving the pastor's house, I officially broke away from Mormonism. I didn't realize it at the time, but everyone I knew was in the Mormon Church. Breaking away was hard for me because it had been my whole world, the only place where people would take care of me or talk with me. When you leave the Mormon Church, you lose everyone and everything – but I remembered the verse in the Bible where Jesus says, "Everyone who has left houses or brothers or sisters or father or mother or wife or children or fields for My sake will receive a hundred times as much and will inherit eternal life" (Matthew 19:29, NIV).

I didn't go to church for a long time after that. I was already suspicious and hurt from my long tenure at the Mormon Church, and a while after I moved out of the pastor's house, his wife yelled and cursed at me on the phone, blaming me for her marriage problems. After that interaction, I thought, "If Christians are like this, I don't want to be a Christian." But my belief was on a more solid footing than it had been in the past, and God was patient with me. Over time He showed me that Christians don't think they're better than everyone else; they know they are so broken that if they don't have a Savior they can't be with God.

Christians… were just like me.

I was still full of anxiety and had so many questions, but throughout all this time, God was kind. He'd speak to me as I got my first job at Denny's, encouraging me not to withdraw, retreat, and quit like I wanted to do. I learned to hold onto John 14:1 where it says not to let your heart be troubled. My natural response to conflict was to run and hide, but I learned that there was a better way.

Eventually, I started going to church again – but a real, Christian church called Foothills where people loved me and loved God. It's been such a warm and loving place to gather with God's children.

I'm 42 years old today, and my life's problems weren't all solved in an instant. I had to go from the edge of death to just suicidal, from suicidal to severely depressed, from severely depressed to chronically depressed, and then finally to peace. I'm learning joy now. When I think and talk about my Jesus and all that He's done for me and all that He's rescued me from, it makes me cry, but they're happy tears.

I was damaged. I've left out most of the details, but that fact remains the same. I was really, really damaged, but God sought me out and bought me anyway. I don't live in despair or suicidal thoughts or depression anymore. I like life! I love life, and I see God's beauty, purpose, and handiwork every-where.

Now, my life is defined by two things: I always wanted to be loved, and I found out that Jesus cherishes me.

He loves me, and if you let Him and don't give up, there's no depression He can't love you out of either.

Cindy Petretta

"There Is Peace"

I grew up in church, but I wasn't there when I needed it the most.

To be honest, I think it was a legalistic thing for me. I did all of the camps and events and everything, but I wasn't passionate about the truth. I had a lot of anger underneath the surface that I didn't understand back then, so even though I was on the straight and narrow all through high school, by college I had started to fall away.

I went to church less and less often, I got distracted by other pursuits, and my new friends weren't encouraging me to continue following Christ. Still, things seemed like they were under control, until my senior year when I found out that I was pregnant.

It wasn't planned, of course, and suddenly things were definitely not under control.

My friends told me to get an abortion, but that was out of the question for me. I was terrified to tell my family, expecting a lot of judgment. I had no idea what to do, so like any rational adult – I ignored it. Well, that strategy only worked for so long. Finally, there I was, four months pregnant and unable to keep avoiding contact or pretending that I'd just gained a few pounds. I was clearly pregnant, and something had to change.

I remember sitting in my car, trying to figure out what I was going to do, when a song came on the Christian radio station. I can't even remember what song it was, but at the time it was like a message from heaven. Suddenly I had this peace, like everything was going to be alright. I knew that my life was going to change forever, but it didn't have to be devastation. I would just have to walk down a different path than the one I had thought.

I told my family, and it was embarrassing but definitely not as bad as I thought. No one yelled at me, and I was accepted. The baby came into the world, and I named him Jordan.

My boyfriend (the baby's father) and I were encouraged to get married to make things right. We did, but things didn't seem right. My husband was not a Christian, and without going into a lot of detail, the marriage did not last. When my son was three years old, my husband and I divorced, fairly amicably.

From that point, my life was really about my son Jordan. We were somewhat involved in a church, but I kept myself pretty disconnected from relationships of all types. I felt ashamed to be around my family, because they were a bunch of heroes serving in the police department, and I was just a single mom trying to pay the bills each month. I had finally graduated from college (three years after getting pregnant), and as a recently-divorced mom of a toddler, I just put my head down and worked, making sure to spend as much time as possible with my son.

This was my life for a while, and though some parts of it were difficult, it was bearable. I felt like I was in control again.

Even better, by the time my son was nine years old, I met a Christian man at work. He was sweet and interesting and kind, and he was intentional in building a relationship with my son and me. A year later we got married, and then everything changed.

It was like I woke up, and I'd married a different man than the one I'd been dating. He became extremely volatile, and I'm going to skip a lot of the details, but suffice it to say, it was not a healthy home for my son or me to be in. To complicate things even more, I'd gotten pregnant almost as soon as we were married – a honeymoon baby. So being pregnant made these new issues that much scarier.

Then one day, my son and I returned from an outing, and my husband was gone.

The furniture was cleared out, all of his things were gone, and not so much as a word of goodbye. To be honest, we were sort of relieved, but being left alone with Jordan and two months pregnant in a new house that I suddenly couldn't afford – that was scary.

I wasn't worried about the money for some

reason. I had trust in God for that, and I knew somehow we'd be okay. But I knew I didn't have control over my life again, and that scared me. At work, things were so awkward. How do you respond when someone who knows your ex-husband that you only married two and a half months ago says, "Hey, how's married life?" What's even worse is that we had already announced the baby, so once the gossip got around about what had happened, people just stared at me with a sad look on their faces. It was embarrassing, and so I pulled back from people again. It was lonely, but I had my kids to think of.

I was extremely stressed and anxious. Every day I was running on high alert, just trying to make everything work. I was pregnant but I was losing weight instead of gaining it, which is very un-healthy for the baby. I wanted this little girl so badly, but in my mind, I tried to prepare for the worst, because how could such a tiny thing survive with the way my body was handling the stress?
And just when things couldn't get any worse, they did.

My ex-husband, who I had not heard a peep from since he left, was suing me for custody of the child I was still pregnant with. It was a very contentious court battle that would end up lasting for years.

Forty weeks to the day after my wedding day, I gave birth to my daughter Evan. Thankfully, she was healthy. Unfortunately, three weeks into my maternity leave, I got a call from the HR department at my work telling me that I was being laid off as part of a company-wide reduction in personnel.

So there I was, with no job, about to lose my medical insurance at the time when I needed it the most, and I had a mortgage and two kids to provide for. I was a mess. I was riddled with anxiety, hardly sleeping, and the judge in our custody case ordered that I had to hand over my one-month-old baby to my ex-husband for 24 hours on Christmas Day.

Jordan and I had a short Christmas together on Christmas morning, and then he had to go to his dad's. Then, someone showed up to take my new daughter away from me – my daughter who was breastfeeding and needed her mother. And I sat on the floor, entirely, completely alone. I literally watched the clock the entire day, counting the hours until I got my baby back. I was so miserable, so lonely, so out of control and anxious. I was angry at the court system, and I was angry at God.

This, finally, was rock bottom.

I was shocked at my own animosity. I wept and shouted at God. I am not a person who shows a lot of emotion, but it was all coming out that day. I cried out, "Why, God? I keep being gracious and trusting You as much as I can, and I expected You to fight for me! Where is my justice? Why haven't You defended me from this?"

I deflated, then. All of the fight went out of me, and I found myself in a pile on the floor, when a Christian song came to my mind. It says:

What if Your blessings come through raindrops?
What if Your healing comes through tears?
*What if a thousand sleepless nights are what it takes to
know You're near?*

It must have been the Holy Spirit, because all of a sudden I had peace. I hadn't had that in a long time, but it was like I released something to God. I could become bitter and crazy, or I could let it go, trust God, and move on. I was struggling, but I believed what God says in the Bible, that He could bring good out of this whole mess. I decided that I would trust Him, even if I wasn't the one in control of things.

I didn't have any friends – I felt embarrassed to be this new mom walking around with a newborn and no husband. I didn't feel like I could relate to the other Little League moms of eleven-year-olds. I was distant from my family because they were so angry at my ex-husband for what he had done, and any time I saw them, they wanted to rant about it, which was just rehashing all of the old hurts.

But I had decided that I was going to try and trust God, and at a certain point I realized that meant I needed to be serious about pursuing God and being part of His Church.

I found a mentor at Foothills, then another. I started signing up for all of the classes I could find, because I was desperate to learn and draw closer to God. I walked into a Sunday morning class taught by Jeff and Roxanne Fulkerson one morning without knowing the topic – and when they started, it was of course about forgiveness. I had to laugh to myself. "I see what you're doing, God." It was a very helpful time, and I learned a lot.

I tried to get involved with women's groups at the church, even though I was intimidated. What could these picture-perfect women with no problems and no worries possible have to do with me? As I started overcoming my own prejudices, I found that a lot of people had issues too, and they weren't judgmental of me. I found some of my best friends in these women's groups.

Healing was slow, but being on that road was so different than living in the bitterness, loneliness, and fear. God held my hand every step of the way and taught me that even when I was grievously wronged, I could forgive. Even when I felt so alone, Jesus was sitting beside me, weeping too. Even when I was out of control, God was still in control.

Life is hard. There is suffering. But when we surrender to the goodness of God, life can be sweet, too. There is joy. There is peace.

I don't have time to go into all of the many ways God provided for me and my kids over the years. I didn't lose my house. I have a wonderful job with strange hours, which allows me to spend a lot of time with my kids.

There are a lot of things that I wish I hadn't had to go through, but I am glad for them, in a way. God's blessings did come through raindrops, like the song says. My two children are the best part of my life. The hardships and betrayals I experienced finally showed me that I needed God. Once I could admit to really needing Him, I could submit to Him, and that was healing.

I still have struggles, but God is in the driver's seat now. I guess He always was.

Chris and Lindsay Flintjer

"Delivered from Drugs"

Lindsay: My dad was a drug addict. I was raised by my mom, and I always, since I was a kid, just had the understanding that I would be a drug addict like my dad. I started using when I was in junior high.

Chris: I came from a relatively good family. My parents loved me, but I was able to do pretty much whatever I wanted. When I was a teenager, I started using drugs – just drinking, smoking weed in high school, partying… That eventually led to heavier drugs. When I was 21 years old, my father passed away, and I didn't know how to handle it. I didn't know what to do with the emotions, and that kind of led me to using heroin. I could use that and not have to think about my dad being gone. It took my mind off of it. That was the beginning of a downhill spiral.

Lindsay: We met through mutual friends, partying. We were attracted to each other. He was funny.

Chris: And she was good looking.

Lindsay: So that's how we met. We immediately started using drugs together, and we were just party buddies. We were using heroin for about four years, every day, all day. And we eventually got arrested.

Chris: She was released. I had to go to jail for a while. Part of my deal for getting out was that I had to go to Restoration Ranch, which is a program to help people get off and stay off of drugs and alcohol. It's a Christian program, so while I was there, the seed was planted. I didn't know much about God before, and I wasn't into hearing about it then, but that seed stayed in my heart somewhere.

Around the time I got out of the Ranch, our first son, King, was born. And Lindsay and I were living together again, clean, but after six months went by we were using again. It didn't take long before, instead of just using heroin, now we were using meth too. We started mixing them, and our lives started getting really crazy.

Lindsay: That's just all we did was use drugs together and fight. Arguing, screaming…

Chris: We didn't know how to communicate. Every disagreement was a big fight. We'd call each other names, scream, and threaten to leave each other. Our relationship was everything you wouldn't want it to be at that time.

Lindsay: Chris got his seed of faith from that first stay at Restoration Ranch, but God planted the seed in my heart from our drug dealers. They were living with us at the time, and they had been Christians before they relapsed back into an addiction lifestyle. I saw something in them, a unity, that even in their broken and backslidden state, was different than any other relationship I'd ever seen, and I wanted it. I started reading the Bible, then – I was just completely high while I was doing it.

Our drug use got so bad, that I actually dropped off my infant son with my mother-in-law so I could go off and do more drugs. I felt horrible about it. I wanted to be with my son, but I kept feeding my addiction instead, and the addiction was fed because I wanted to forget how bad of a mother I was being. I couldn't take enough drugs to forget my son. Every time I started coming down from a high, I'd start thinking about him again, and I'd feel tormented inside.

I eventually did enough drugs to actually go insane, and I ended up in the hospital. That is where, I believe, the Lord delivered me from my desire to use drugs. I had sobriety all of a sudden, because of the hospital stay, and it's like my mind was cleared to accept all of what I had been reading in the Bible and trying to learn about God. I can't pinpoint an exact moment, but I just know that I left the hospital with no desire to use ever again.

Chris: We found out that we were pregnant with

baby number two, and I wanted nothing more than to be there with Lindsay and our kids, but I was stuck on the world. I was stuck in my addiction, and that's what I pursued. I wound up in jail, and that enabled my mind to clear up a little bit. So when they released me, I chose to go back to Restoration Ranch, this time of my own free will. I wanted to get my life back in order. During the few months I was there, my wife and I got baptized, along with my mom, and I came home and started working.

I had one more relapse. I'd left the Ranch too early, and I fell back into my addiction, but it was different this time because now, I was the Lord's. I had given my life to Him, but I couldn't make the right decisions to follow Him well. I kept making the wrong decisions. Well, He wouldn't let any of my old connections or back-up plans work. It wasn't the good time I used to think that it was. I ended up homeless, without even a couch to sleep on.

Lindsay: I didn't know where he was for months. Family members told me, "Thank goodness that guy is out of your life. Move on and don't look back." But even then, I was committed to Chris. He and I were always committed to each other even when we were totally immature, making a mess of our lives, and hurting each other. He was the father of my children, and I decided I was going to just pray for him and wait for the Lord to bring him back.

Chris: I ended up back in jail, again, which was the biggest blessing ever. My mind cleared up in there, and I cried out to God every day. There was a night that came up where I was doing that, and I had my Bible on my chest, and I was praying. I felt this weight around my heart, like I could physically feel it, and the Lord just lifted it. He took it off of me, and I literally felt like I was floating – totally sober at this time. Along with that weight being lifted off of me went all the fear and anxiety that I had, and I knew at that point that everything was going to be okay. And everything was, from then on.

I went back to Restoration Ranch, this time deciding to stay for six months to a year. When I was up there, Lindsay and I started going to Foothills Church every week, and since then, we haven't stopped.

Lindsay: So we were not married yet, but we had three kids. We were committed to each other, but Chris and I lived apart. We were Christians, but we didn't know how to live in God's ways beyond trying not to go back to drugs and trying to be present for each other and our kids.

Chris: It was much better than when we were using, but Lindsay and I still fought all the time. We didn't know how to communicate. The way I was raised and had chosen to live my life, I was all about me. I would work for a while, then lose my job and not really care. I wasn't a good provider, and I didn't understand why I had to be.

Lindsay: And I was raised on power-feminism, and the way I had chosen to live my life up to that point was making everything about my choices and what I wanted to do. So that makes for a tough relationship when a man doesn't want to lead and a woman doesn't want to follow. The world taught us how to live, and in everyday life it just turned out to be insufficient.

Chris: We started learning from the church. Foothills really taught us God's Word and how to live our lives like God intended, and our relationship started to get better.

Lindsay: We were going to marriage counseling to work out our problems, where it was suggested that we get married, which was a great idea. We didn't have a lot of money at the time, so we got married in room A-1 at the church. And I really feel like from that point on, the Lord really blessed us.

Chris: We were living in a one-room studio in Ramona with our three kids at that point, and once we got married, it was like God was able to pour out His blessings on our family and our lives, because we had submitted to His design. We were able to rent an awesome house with a big yard for the kids to play in even though we definitely did not meet the financial qualifications that they wanted applicants to have. I learned about being a good husband and man, and my wife does a great job being a wife and a woman. We learned a new way of doing everything.

Lindsay: We were much different people back when we met, and since we've become more of who the Lord wants us to be, we've fallen in love again as these new people.

Chris: It's a miracle. We fell in love twice.

Lindsay: A lot of couples that use together don't make it through changes with their relationship lasting, but I feel like because of God, because we started pursuing Him first, He has just blessed our lives so much.

Dylan Morris

"The Lord Took Me In"

I didn't have the best home life growing up.

My parents were usually sleeping or busy. They had strangers over all the time, and they were wrapped up in substance abuse. No one really had time for me, and I didn't have a lot of basic needs taken care of – clean clothes, food, etc. When I was younger, I just thought that's how life was. Kids at school would say, "Who woke up on the wrong side of the bed?" or "Why do you smell so bad?" and I didn't like it, but I shrugged it off. It was all I'd ever known.

My family situation got tougher. When I was in the seventh grade, we became homeless. That meant that my mom, my dad, my brother Travis, my sister Ashley, and I all had to live in a van. My brother Kyle had found somewhere else to live, but I missed him. It was crowded in the van, embarrassing to be living this way, and if I thought that things couldn't get any worse from there, I was wrong.

But I had something good to hold onto, a lifeline. When I was in the fifth grade, my brother Kyle started going to this place called Youth Venture. It was run by Foothills Church, but what I liked about it was that there were video games, there was free food, and it was someplace to hang out that wasn't home. I was too young to be going, but I thought I'd just slip in under the age requirement.

One day I was at Youth Venture, and Danny Eslinger, who was the director at the time, came up to me and asked how old I was. I told him that I was in the sixth grade – which was how old you had to be to come. Danny looked at me and said, "No… I don't think you're in sixth grade. You look too young to be here." I insisted that I really was how old I said I was, so Danny came up with a compromise. "If your hand is bigger than your face, then you're in sixth grade," he said. So I put my hand over my face, and he gently bopped it, and we laughed. "You're not old enough to be here," he said. He was nice about it so I couldn't be angry. I nodded and turned to go, when he stopped me. "But I want you to stay," he added.

This was the first time I'd ever really felt wanted, other than the occasional invite from my brother to hang out with him. It was huge for me.

I started going to Youth Venture every day, and I wasn't into the Bible lessons or the talk about God, but I really appreciated the people and their love for me. Youth Venture was there for me when we became homeless, and they were there when things got worse.

By the time I was in the seventh grade, like I mentioned before, we had been living in the van, and I was spending as much time at Youth Venture as I could. One day my dad stopped by the center to find me. He told me, "The van got impounded. I know where I'm going to stay, but I don't know where you're going to stay." Then he left.

Needless to say, that was terrible. It was bad enough that we were poor, it was bad enough that there were drugs, that we were homeless, that I had dirty clothes, and my parents' marriage was falling apart, but then my dad basically told me that I was on my own. No one should have to hear that as a kid.

The leaders at Youth Venture were there for me. They were like God's ambassadors in my life. I started going to church at Foothills, my brother Kyle came back with the intent of helping me navigate these hard times and come to God.

I was resistant to the Jesus message for a long time. I just liked to be around the people.

A few years later, as the youth conference Future Quest was coming up, Pastor Mark Hoffman pulled me aside and asked me if I planned to go.

I had never wanted to go to Future Quest in all of the past years. Sure, it seemed like a lot of fun and a bunch of my friends were going – but I didn't have the money to sign up, and I was embarrassed to ask for help.

I told Mark that I didn't want to go. He very kindly said that he would pay for my admission, and I still said no. Then he said that he wanted me to go, and I finally relented. Mark had been a good person to me, and I wanted to do right by him. Secretly, I did want to see Future Quest, but once I got there, God met me in a way I never expected.

Pastor Bill Wilson shared his testimony on the last night of the conference. He told us how his mother left him on a street corner. She abandoned him as a little kid, and he sat on the corner for three days. He would have died, except a Christian man came by and noticed that this same kid was always in the same spot, so he took him in. Pastor Bill said that no matter who's left you behind, God wants you. God loves you. He encouraged us to give our lives to Jesus, and I just found myself on my feet walking to the altar. I got saved that night, and life has never been the same since.

I have a good job today, a beautiful wife, and our first child was just born. His home life is going to be a lot different than mine was, and that's all because of Christ. God not only changed my life – the ripples of His love that He showed me through the people of Youth Venture will affect my son and hopefully every generation to come.

I was abandoned, like Pastor Bill, and the Lord took me in.

If you are struggling with anxiety, depression, hard financial circumstances, or any other hardship, know that the church is here to help and provide the love of Christ. No one should walk alone.

Foothills Christian Church Office:
(619) 442-7728
Receptionist@foothillschurch.org

Foothills Christian Church Counseling Office:
(619) 442-7728 (ask for Counseling)
Counseling@foothillschurch.org

Church Office
350 Cypress Lane, Ste. B
El Cajon, CA 92020

Sanctuary
365 W. Bradley Ave.
El Cajon, CA 92020